Learning

Three-Octave Scales

on the Cello

by Cassia Harvey

CHP356

©2019 by C. Harvey Publications All Rights Reserved.

www.learnstrings.com - downloadable books
www.charveypublications.com - print books

Table of Contents

Section	Page
How This Book Works	2
How to Use This Book	3
About the Thumb	4
Using Whole and Half Steps in This Book	5

Part One: Learning the Major Scales

C major	8
G major	12
D major	16
A major	20
E major	24
B major	28
F-sharp major	32
D-flat major	36
A-flat major	40
E-flat major	44
B-flat major	48
F major	52

Part Two: Learning the Minor Scales

A melodic minor	56
A harmonic minor	60
E melodic minor	62
E harmonic minor	66
B melodic minor	68
B harmonic minor	72
F-sharp melodic minor	74
F-sharp harmonic minor	78
C-sharp melodic minor	80
C-sharp harmonic minor	84
G-sharp melodic minor	86
G-sharp harmonic minor	90
E-flat melodic minor	92
E-flat harmonic minor	96
B-flat melodic minor	98
B-flat harmonic minor	102
F melodic minor	104
F harmonic minor	108
C melodic minor	110
C harmonic minor	114
G melodic minor	116
G harmonic minor	120
D melodic minor	122
D harmonic minor	126

Part Three: Learning a Chromatic Scale	128
Part Four: Scales to Memorize	134
What Comes Next	143

©2019 C. Harvey Publications All Rights Reserved.

How This Book Works

• Each scale is taught using spacing exercises and shifting exercises.

• When you see this figure, a **space** between two notes is being taught:

• The **shifts** are taught through a variety of exercises that *use notes you already know to help you find the new notes*. In this example, by playing third finger, you can see and hear how far to shift.

• Fourth finger is sometimes used in a high position to show you where to shift. While these notes are awkward to play, they can be very helpful in learning fingerboard geography. Even if your fourth finger can't comfortably reach the note, attempting to play it can still help you see where to shift:

• When there is a clef change in the exercises, the note is written once in each clef so you can see the relationship between the notes and clefs.

• Extra notes are often included to help you hear whether or not you are in the correct position and playing in tune. *Harmonics* and *double stops* are the most common intonation tools used in this book. Match the note you are playing to the open string or harmonic as exactly as possible whenever these notes occur.

Here is an example of a high D that should be played with an open D to check your intonation. Since the low D is written so low in treble clef, words are included to help you recognize open D.

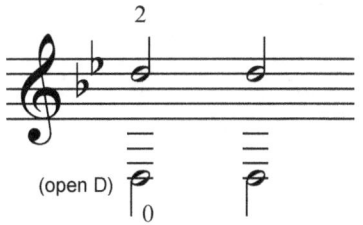

Here is an example of a harmonic that can be used to help you check your intonation. As you press your finger down after the harmonic, listen to hear that the regular note matches the harmonic.

©2019 C. Harvey Publications All Rights Reserved.

How to Use This Book

- Study four pages at a time to learn each major and melodic minor scale and two pages at a time to learn each harmonic minor scale.

- As you practice, focus on remembering both the physical spaces on the fingerboard and the correct sounds of the scale.

- Repeat shifts until they are played precisely and perfectly in tune. Since you are teaching yourself the spaces with quite a bit of repetition, be very careful to place your fingers correctly so that you don't inadvertently build bad habits.

- **Some of the exercises and scales might be most helpful when played with a drone.** The root note, or first note of the scale, is typically the most helpful note to use as a drone. There are apps and websites that have drones to play with; search for *music practice drone*.

- The scales are not written in the book in order of difficulty. If you would like to study the scales in order of difficulty, the list below can help.

Here are the Major Keys Listed in (Approximate) Order of Difficulty

Note: Since not everyone finds the same things difficult, this order is general and not exact and it can be changed to fit your playing.

1. C major
2. D major
3. G major
4. F major
5. A major
6. E-flat major
7. B-flat major
8. E major
9. A-flat major
10. D-flat major
11. B major
12. F-sharp major

Here are the Minor Keys Listed in (Approximate) Order of Difficulty

Note: Since not everyone finds the same things difficult, this order is general and not exact and it can be changed to fit your playing.

1. C melodic and harmonic minor
2. D melodic and harmonic minor
3. G melodic and harmonic minor
4. A melodic and harmonic minor
5. E melodic and harmonic minor
6. B melodic and harmonic minor
7. C-sharp melodic and harmonic minor
8. E-flat melodic and harmonic minor
9. F melodic and harmonic minor
10. F-sharp melodic and harmonic minor
11. G-sharp melodic and harmonic minor
12. B-flat melodic and harmonic minor

©2019 C. Harvey Publications All Rights Reserved.

About the Thumb

While notes that use the thumb are not played in traditional three-octave scales, the position of the thumb is still quite important.

In the lower positions, the thumb should be placed between 1st and 2nd finger in closed positions and under the 2nd finger in extended positions.

In the upper positions, the thumb should be resting lightly on the fingerboard behind the first finger.

The signs that indicate when to bring the thumb up onto and down off of the fingerboard are listed below.

> Note: to avoid unnecessary clutter on the already crowded pages in this book, signs suggesting where to bring the thumb up are only given under the scales themselves and not under the exercises.

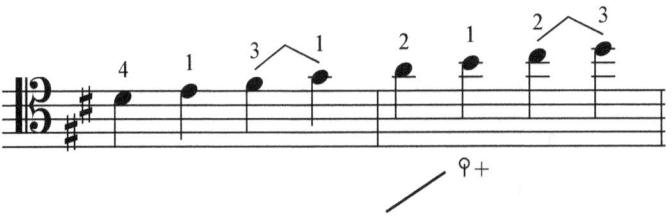

This tells you to bring the thumb up onto the fingerboard, behind the fingers.

Here is a picture of the thumb resting on the string behind the fingers.

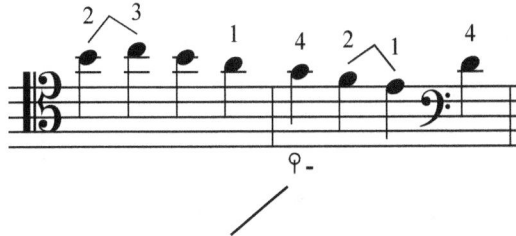

This sign tells you to bring the thumb back down, under the neck.

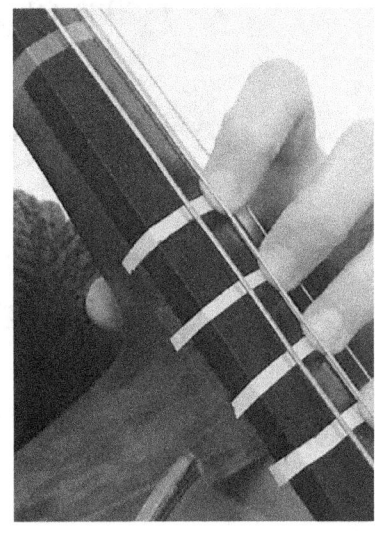

Here is a picture of the thumb back under the neck.

©2019 C. Harvey Publications All Rights Reserved.

Half Steps and Whole Steps: The Building Blocks of Scales

- Western music is based on a system of whole and half steps (also called tones and semitones) that, when put together in a specific way, form a scale.
- Below are the spaces that make up the scales in this book. Starting with the first note in the scale, you could figure out how to play scales anywhere on the cello by playing the steps indicated.
- While you can play scales with any one finger or any combination of fingers, in this book there is only one fingering taught for each three-octave scale. This is to allow you to learn and memorize the scales completely.

Major Scale

first note | whole step | whole step | half step | whole step | whole step | whole step | half step

Melodic Minor Scale

going up the scale

first note | whole step | half step | whole step | whole step | whole step | whole step | half step

coming down the scale

whole step | whole step | half step | whole step | whole step | half step | whole step

Harmonic Minor Scale

first note | whole step | half step | whole step | whole step | half step | 1 1/2 steps | half step

Chromatic Scale

first note | half step | half step | half step | half step | half step | half step | half step | half step | half step | half step | half step | half step

Playing Half, Whole, and 1 1/2 Steps

Here are some practical ways to think of steps on the cello:

•The space between each finger in the regular (closed) lower positions is a half step.

•The space between three fingers (for instance 1st finger and 3rd finger) in regular (closed) lower positions is a whole step.

•To reach a whole step with 1st and 2nd fingers, you must extend or stretch. In this case, the thumb should move up under 2nd finger to allow you to reach easily.

•As you move up through the positions, the spaces between the notes get smaller. A half step in first position will be much bigger than a half step in seventh position.

•In the higher positions, both whole and half steps can be played by any two adjacent fingers (for instance 2nd and 3rd finger). Think of the half steps as "small spaces" and the whole steps as "big spaces" to help differentiate between the two.

•Harmonic minor scales have spaces of 1 1/2 steps. To reach these spaces, you may pivot your hand forward (toward the bridge) to reach the notes. Do not strain your hand to try to reach this difficult stretch. It is much better to release the finger of the previous note before reaching the 1 1/2-step space if there is any strain at all.

Half steps are marked this way:

Half step space

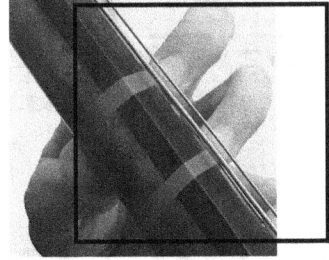

In this book, whole steps are marked this way:

Whole step space with 1st and 3rd finger (closed postiion.)

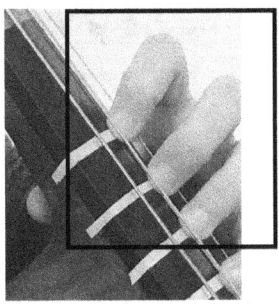

Whole step space with 1st and 2nd finger (extended position.)

©2019 C. Harvey Publications All Rights Reserved.

Part One: Learning the Major Scales
C Major Scale

Cassia Harvey

©2019 C. Harvey Publications All Rights Reserved.

Learning Three-Octave Scales on the Cello　　　　　　　　　　　　　　　　　　　　C Major Scale　9

Learning the Third Octave - Part One

©2019 C. Harvey Publications All Rights Reserved.

Putting the C Major Scale Together

G Major Scale

Learning Three-Octave Scales on the Cello — G Major Scale — 13

Learning the Third Octave - Part One

G Major Scale
Learning Three-Octave Scales on the Cello
Learning the Third Octave - Part Two

©2019 C. Harvey Publications All Rights Reserved.

Learning Three-Octave Scales on the Cello
G Major Scale 15

Putting the G Major Scale Together

G major scale - three octaves

Note: The signs under the notes indicate possible places to move the thumb on and off of the fingerboard during the scale. The thumb is used to stabilize the left hand and lightly balances on the string, shifting with the hand. See page 5 for more explanantion of the thumb indications.

This sign tells you to bring the thumb up onto the fingerboard, behind the fingers: ♀+

This sign tells you to bring the thumb back down, under the neck: ♀-

©2019 C. Harvey Publications All Rights Reserved.

Learning Three-Octave Scales on the Cello — D Major Scale — 17

Learning the Third Octave - Part One

©2019 C. Harvey Publications All Rights Reserved.

D Major Scale

Learning the Third Octave - Part Two

Learning Three-Octave Scales on the Cello — D Major Scale

Putting the D Major Scale Together

©2019 C. Harvey Publications All Rights Reserved.

Learning Three-Octave Scales on the Cello   A Major Scale   21

Learning the Second and Third Octaves

Putting the A Major Scale Together

Learning Three-Octave Scales on the Cello — E Major Scale — 25

Learning the Second Octave

©2019 C. Harvey Publications All Rights Reserved.

E Major Scale

Learning the Second and Third Octaves

Learning Three-Octave Scales on the Cello — E Major Scale — 27

Learning the Third Octave

Third Octave

E major scale - three octaves

©2019 C. Harvey Publications All Rights Reserved.

B Major Scale

Learning the Second Octave

Learning Three-Octave Scales on the Cello — B Major Scale

B Major Scale

Learning Three-Octave Scales on the Cello

Learning the Second and Third Octaves

©2019 C. Harvey Publications All Rights Reserved.

Learning Three-Octave Scales on the Cello — B Major Scale — 31

Putting the B Major Scale together

©2019 C. Harvey Publications All Rights Reserved.

F♯ Major Scale

Learning Three-Octave Scales on the Cello F# Major Scale 33

Learning the Second Octave

©2019 C. Harvey Publications All Rights Reserved.

F# Major Scale
Learning the Third Octave

D♭ Major Scale

First Octave

©2019 C. Harvey Publications All Rights Reserved.

Learning Three-Octave Scales on the Cello

D♭ Major Scale

Learning the Second Octave

©2019 C. Harvey Publications All Rights Reserved.

A♭ Major Scale

Learning Three-Octave Scales on the Cello

©2019 C. Harvey Publications All Rights Reserved.

Learning Three-Octave Scales on the Cello — A♭ Major Scale — 41

Learning the Second Octave

A♭ Major Scale
Learning Three-Octave Scales on the Cello
Learning the Third Octave

Learning Three-Octave Scales on the Cello — A♭ Major Scale — 43

Putting the A♭ Major Scale Together

A♭ major scale - three octaves

©2019 C. Harvey Publications All Rights Reserved.

E♭ Major Scale

Learning Three-Octave Scales on the Cello

©2019 C. Harvey Publications All Rights Reserved.

Learning Three-Octave Scales on the Cello — E♭ Major Scale

More of the Second Octave

Learning Three-Octave Scales on the Cello — E♭ Major Scale — 47

Putting the E♭ Major Scale Together

E♭ major scale - three octaves

©2019 C. Harvey Publications All Rights Reserved.

48

Learning Three-Octave Scales on the Cello

B♭ Major Scale

©2019 C. Harvey Publications All Rights Reserved.

Learning Three-Octave Scales on the Cello — B♭ Major Scale

Learning the Second and Third Octaves

B♭ Major Scale
Learning Three-Octave Scales on the Cello
Learning the Third Octave

Third Octave

Learning Three-Octave Scales on the Cello — B♭ Major Scale — 51

Putting the B♭ Major Scale Together

B♭ major scale - three octaves

F Major Scale

Learning Three-Octave Scales on the Cello F Major Scale

Learning the Second and Third Octaves

©2019 C. Harvey Publications All Rights Reserved.

F Major Scale
Learning Three-Octave Scales on the Cello

More of the Third Octave

Learning Three-Octave Scales on the Cello — F Major Scale — 55

Putting the F Major Scale Together

F major scale - three octaves

©2019 C. Harvey Publications All Rights Reserved.

Part Two: Learning the Minor Scales

A Melodic Minor Scale

Focus on Coming Down the A Melodic Minor Scale

A Melodic Minor Scale

Focus on the Lower Octaves

Learning Three-Octave Scales on the Cello — A Melodic Minor Scale

Putting the A Melodic Minor Scale Together

A melodic minor scale - three octaves

©2019 C. Harvey Publications All Rights Reserved.

A Harmonic Minor Scale

©2019 C. Harvey Publications All Rights Reserved.

Learning Three-Octave Scales on the Cello

A Harmonic Minor Scale

Focus on Coming Down the Scale

A harmonic minor scale - three octaves

©2019 C. Harvey Publications All Rights Reserved.

E Melodic Minor Scale

©2019 C. Harvey Publications All Rights Reserved.

Learning Three-Octave Scales on the Cello E Melodic Minor Scale

Focus on Coming Down the Scale

E Melodic Minor Scale

Focus on Spacing in the Scale

Putting the E Melodic Minor Scale Together

E melodic minor scale - three octaves

E Harmonic Minor Scale

©2019 C. Harvey Publications All Rights Reserved.

Learning Three-Octave Scales on the Cello

E Harmonic Minor Scale

Focus on Coming Down the Scale

E harmonic minor scale - three octaves

©2019 C. Harvey Publications All Rights Reserved.

B Melodic Minor Scale

Learning Three-Octave Scales on the Cello — B Melodic Minor Scale — 69

Focus on Spacing in the Scale

©2019 C. Harvey Publications All Rights Reserved.

B Melodic Minor Scale

Focus on Coming Down the Scale

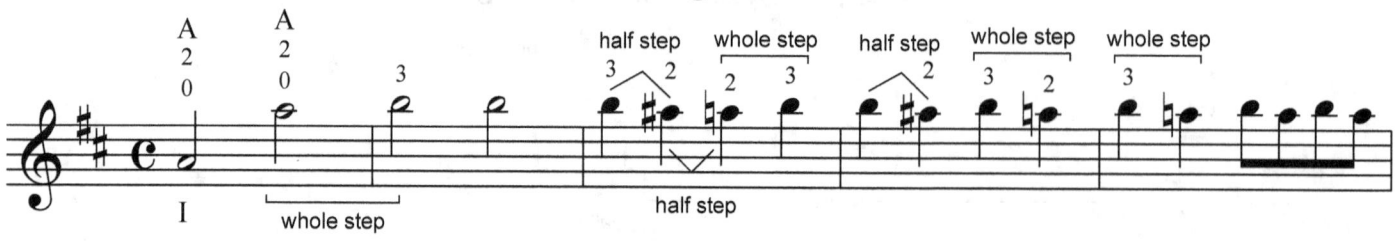
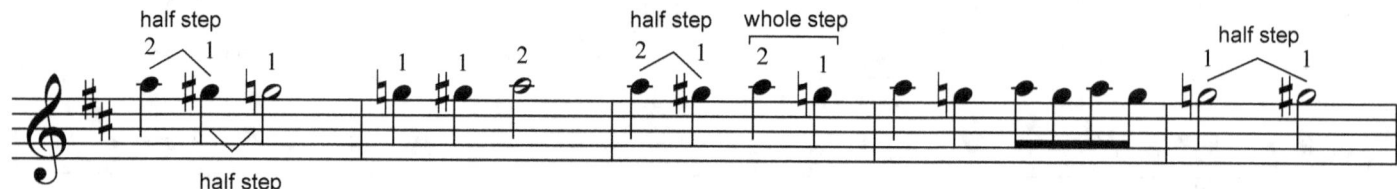

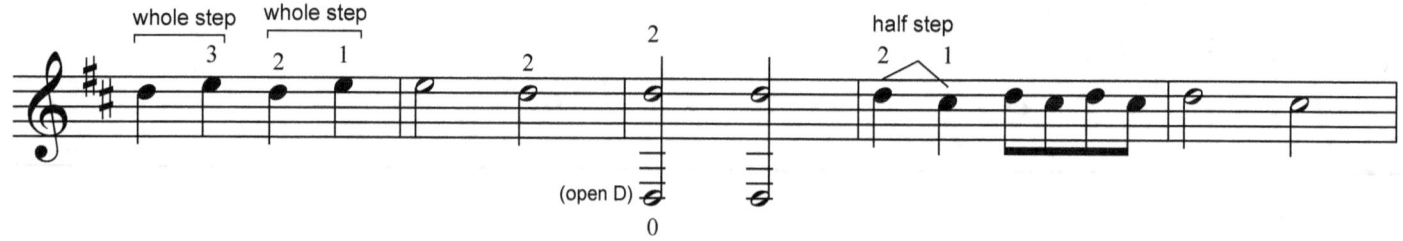

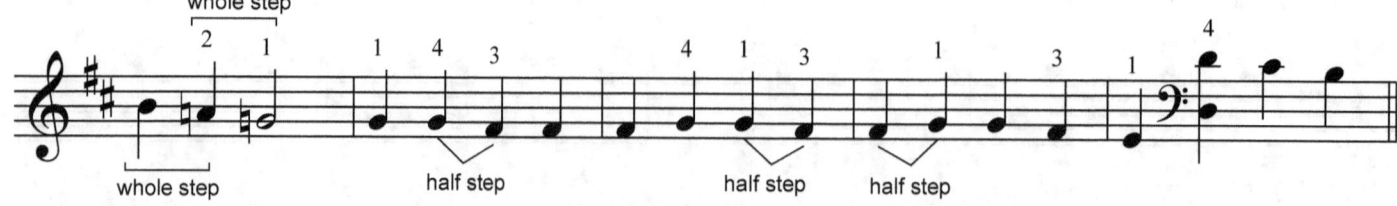

©2019 C. Harvey Publications All Rights Reserved.

Putting the B Melodic Minor Scale Together

B melodic minor scale - three octaves

B Harmonic Minor Scale

Continue on to the next page.

©2019 C. Harvey Publications All Rights Reserved.

B Harmonic Minor Scale, continued

B harmonic minor scale - three octaves

F# Melodic Minor Scale

©2019 C. Harvey Publications All Rights Reserved.

Learning Three-Octave Scales on the Cello F# Melodic Minor Scale 75

Focus on Coming Down the Scale

©2019 C. Harvey Publications All Rights Reserved.

F# Melodic Minor Scale

Focus on the Lower Octaves

Putting the F# Melodic Minor Scale Together

F# melodic minor scale - three octaves

©2019 C. Harvey Publications All Rights Reserved.

F# Harmonic Minor Scale

Continue on to the next page.

Learning Three-Octave Scales on the Cello F# Harmonic Minor Scale 79

F# Harmonic Minor Scale, Continued

F# harmonic minor scale - three octaves

©2019 C. Harvey Publications All Rights Reserved.

C# Melodic Minor Scale

Learning Three-Octave Scales on the Cello — C# Melodic Minor Scale

Focus on Coming Down the Scale

C# Melodic Minor Scale
Focus on the Lower Octaves

Learning Three-Octave Scales on the Cello

C# Melodic Minor Scale

Putting the C# Melodic Minor Scale Together

C# Harmonic Minor Scale

Learning Three-Octave Scales on the Cello — C# Harmonic Minor Scale

Coming Down the C# Harmonic Minor Scale

C# harmonic minor scale - three octaves

©2019 C. Harvey Publications All Rights Reserved.

G♯ Melodic Minor Scale

Learning Three-Octave Scales on the Cello G# Melodic Minor Scale

Focus on the Top Octave

©2019 C. Harvey Publications All Rights Reserved.

G♯ Melodic Minor Scale

Focus on the Lower Octaves

©2019 C. Harvey Publications All Rights Reserved.

Putting the G# Melodic Minor Scale Together

G# melodic minor scale - three octaves

G# Harmonic Minor Scale

©2019 C. Harvey Publications All Rights Reserved.

Learning Three-Octave Scales on the Cello

G♯ Harmonic Minor Scale

Coming Down the G♯ Harmonic Minor Scale

E♭ Melodic Minor Scale

Learning Three-Octave Scales on the Cello — E♭ Melodic Minor Scale

Focus on Coming Down the Scale

E♭ Melodic Minor Scale

Focus on the Lower Octaves

E♭ Harmonic Minor Scale

Learning Three-Octave Scales on the Cello — E♭ Harmonic Minor Scale — 97

Putting the E♭ Harmonic Minor Scale Together

E♭ harmonic minor scale - three octaves

©2019 C. Harvey Publications All Rights Reserved.

B♭ Melodic Minor Scale

Learning Three-Octave Scales on the Cello B♭ Melodic Minor Scale

Focus on Coming Down the Scale

©2019 C. Harvey Publications All Rights Reserved.

B♭ Melodic Minor Scale

Focus on the Lower Octaves

©2019 C. Harvey Publications All Rights Reserved.

Learning Three-Octave Scales on the Cello — B♭ Melodic Minor Scale — 101

Putting the B♭ Melodic Minor Scale Together

B♭ melodic minor scale - three octaves

©2019 C. Harvey Publications All Rights Reserved.

B♭ Harmonic Minor Scale

©2019 C. Harvey Publications All Rights Reserved.

F Melodic Minor Scale

F Melodic Minor Scale

Focus on Coming Down the Scale

F Melodic Minor Scale
Focus on the Lower Octaves

Putting the F Melodic Minor Scale Together

F melodic minor scale - three octaves

F Harmonic Minor Scale

Learning Three-Octave Scales on the Cello

F Harmonic Minor Scale

Coming Down the F Harmonic Minor Scale

F harmonic minor scale - three octaves

C Melodic Minor Scale

Learning Three-Octave Scales on the Cello — C Melodic Minor Scale — 111

Focus on Coming Down the Scale

©2019 C. Harvey Publications All Rights Reserved.

C Melodic Minor Scale

Focus on Learning the Scale

Learning Three-Octave Scales on the Cello — C Melodic Minor Scale — 113

Putting the C Melodic Minor Scale Together

©2019 C. Harvey Publications All Rights Reserved.

C Harmonic Minor Scale

G Melodic Minor Scale

Learning Three-Octave Scales on the Cello

G Melodic Minor Scale

Focus on Coming Down the Scale

©2019 C. Harvey Publications All Rights Reserved.

G Melodic Minor Scale

Focus on Learning the Scale

Putting the G Melodic Minor Scale Together

G melodic minor scale - three octaves

G Harmonic Minor Scale

©2019 C. Harvey Publications All Rights Reserved.

Learning Three-Octave Scales on the Cello — G Harmonic Minor Scale — 121

Coming Down the G Harmonic Minor Scale

G harmonic minor scale - three octaves

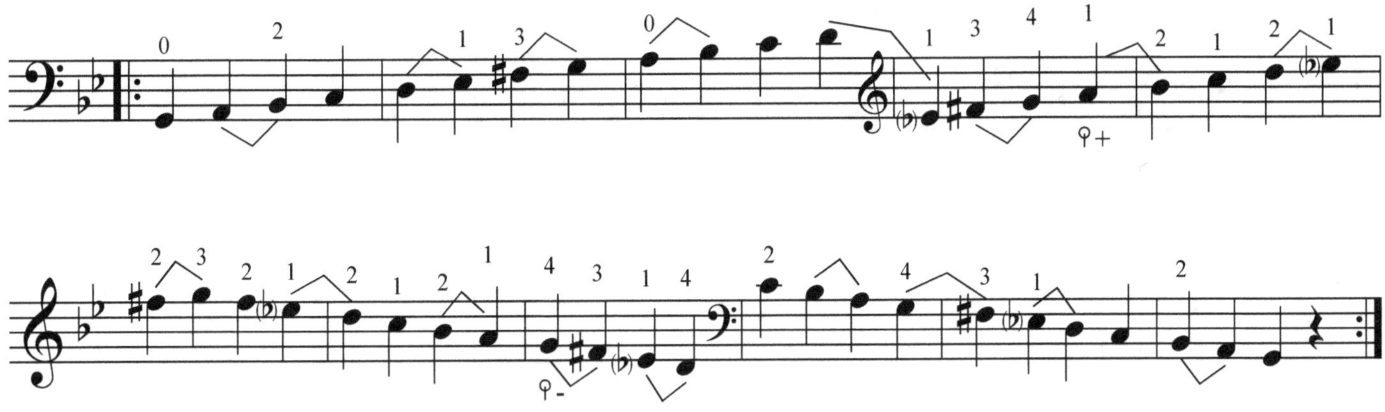

©2019 C. Harvey Publications All Rights Reserved.

D Melodic Minor Scale

Learning Three-Octave Scales on the Cello

D Melodic Minor Scale   123

Focus on Coming Down the Scale

D Melodic Minor Scale

Focus on Learning the Scale

Putting the D Melodic Minor Scale Together

D melodic minor scale - three octaves

D Harmonic Minor Scale

©2019 C. Harvey Publications All Rights Reserved.

Learning Three-Octave Scales on the Cello

Coming Down the D Harmonic Minor Scale

D Harmonic Minor Scale   127

©2019 C. Harvey Publications All Rights Reserved.

Part Three: Learning a Chromatic Scale

A **chromatic scale** consists only of half step spaces. Chromatic scales are useful for learning to hear how chromatic spacing sounds, developing the muscle memory to play entirely in half steps, and preparing for the many chromatic passages in cello literature.

Chromatic Scale: Spacing Exercise

Learning Three-Octave Scales on the Cello — Chromatic Scale

Chromatic Scale: Shifting Exercise No. 1

©2019 C. Harvey Publications All Rights Reserved.

Chromatic Scale: Shifting Exercise No. 2

Chromatic Scale: Intonation Exercise

Part Four: Scales to Memorize

Note: This mark indicates a possible place to move the thumb up onto the fingerboard: ♀+
This mark indicates a possible place to move the thumb back down behind the cello neck: ♀-

C major scale

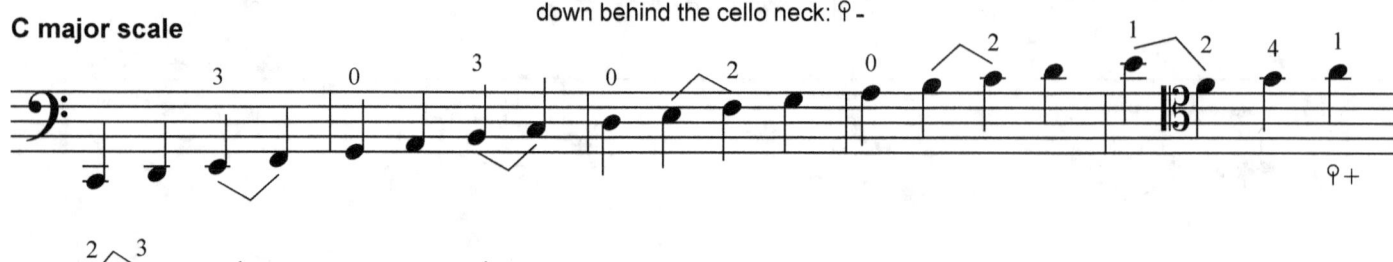

D♭ major scale

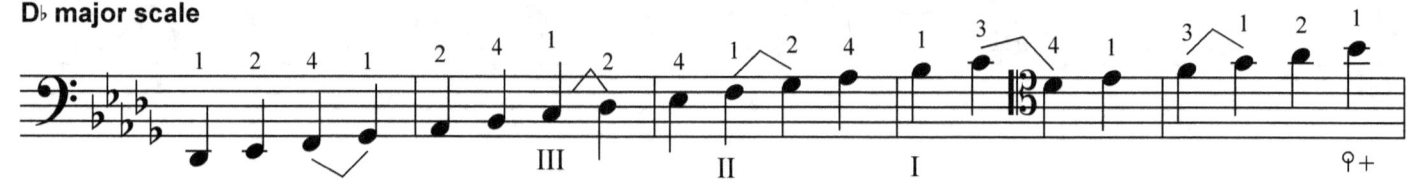

D major scale

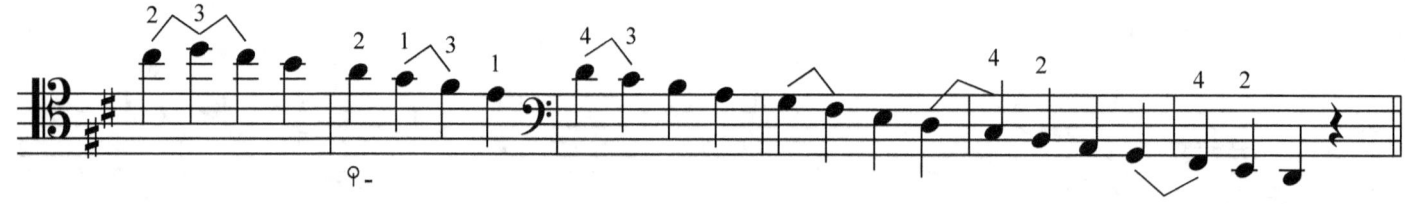

E♭ major scale

©2019 C. Harvey Publications All Rights Reserved.

Learning Three-Octave Scales on the Cello — Major Scales — 135

E major scale

F major scale

F♯ major scale

G major scale

©2019 C. Harvey Publications All Rights Reserved.

Learning Three-Octave Scales on the Cello — Minor Scales — 137

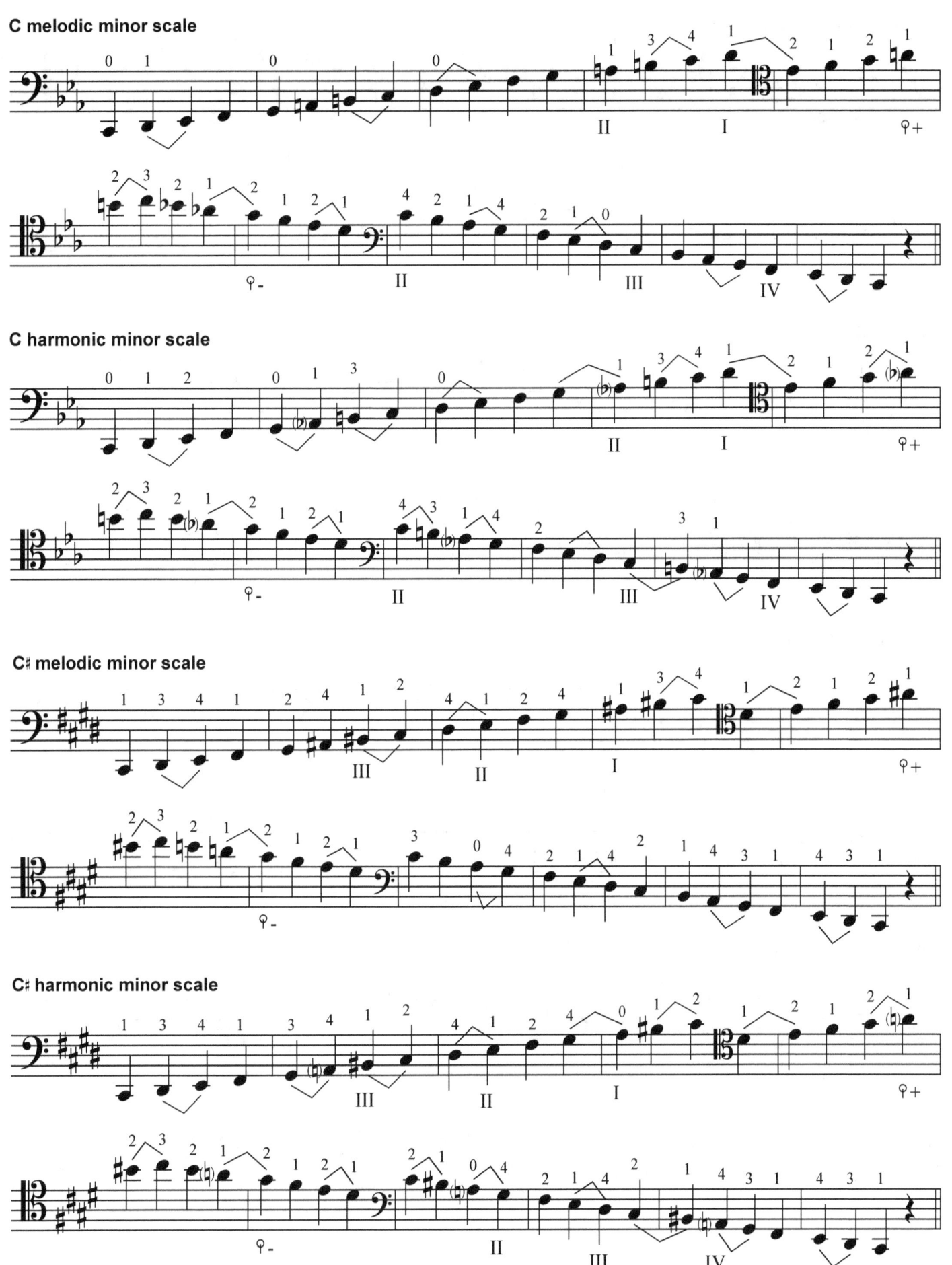

©2019 C. Harvey Publications All Rights Reserved.

Minor Scales

D melodic minor scale

D harmonic minor scale

E♭ melodic minor scale

E♭ harmonic minor scale

Learning Three-Octave Scales on the Cello — Minor Scales — 139

©2019 C. Harvey Publications All Rights Reserved.

Minor Scales

Learning Three-Octave Scales on the Cello

F# melodic minor scale

F# harmonic minor scale

G melodic minor scale

G harmonic minor scale

©2019 C. Harvey Publications All Rights Reserved.

G♯ melodic minor scale

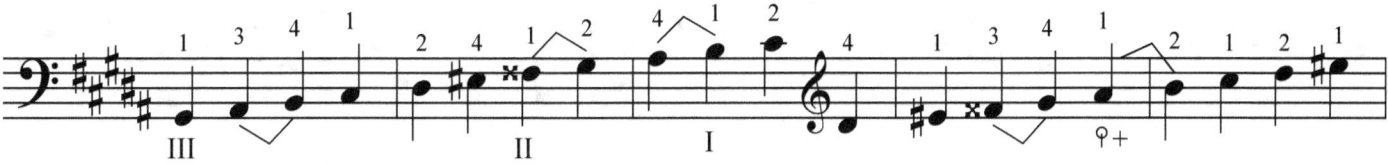

G♯ harmonic minor scale

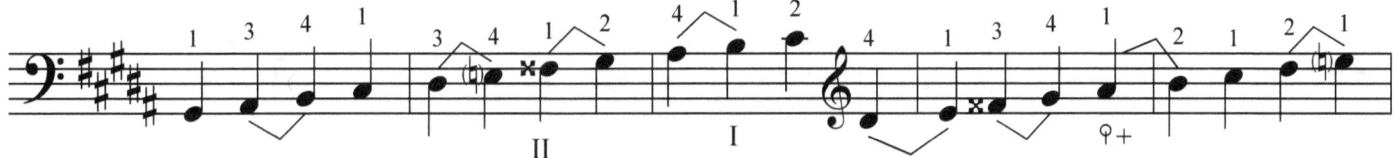

A melodic minor scale

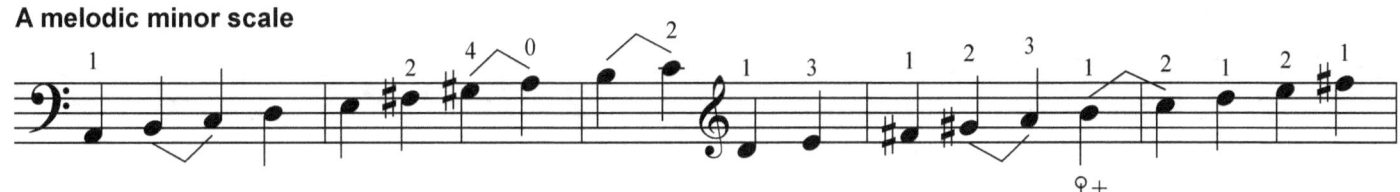
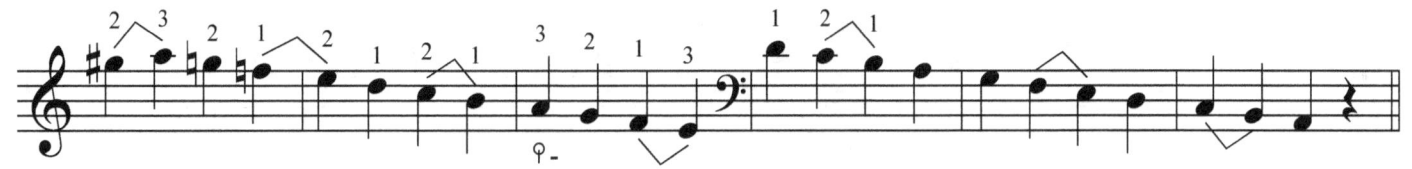

A harmonic minor scale

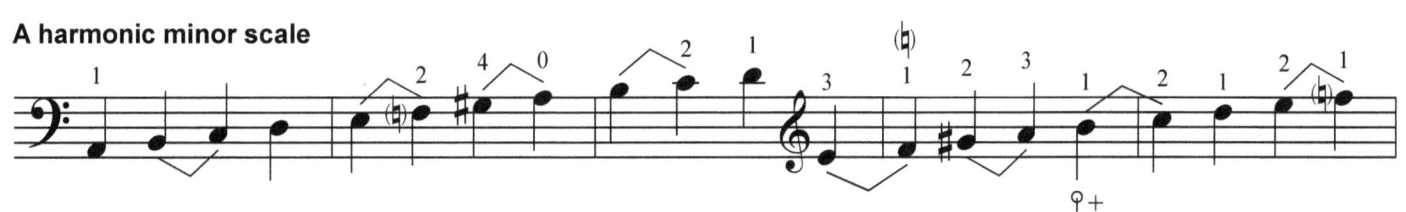
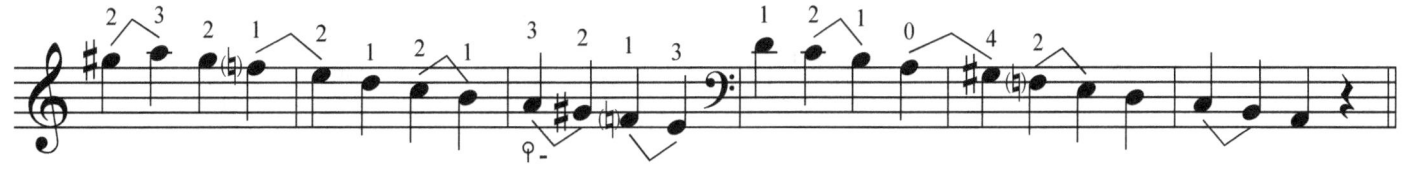

What Comes Next

Learning to play scales is just the beginning! A well-rounded daily practice routine should nearly always include scales in some form. However, just playing scales in quarter or eighth notes limits how much the scales can help you improve.

That's where scale variations are valuable. By practicing rhythm, bow, and note variations on scales, both the left and right hands can be trained at the same time.

When you play variations, your practice becomes more efficient as the scope of the scales is expanded to teach an almost limitless variety of cello techniques.

Here is an overview of some of the scale books you could study next.
All books are available from **www.charveypublications.com**.

The first book in the *Three-Octave Scales* series focuses first on improving shifting and then on playing the scales faster.
CHP152

 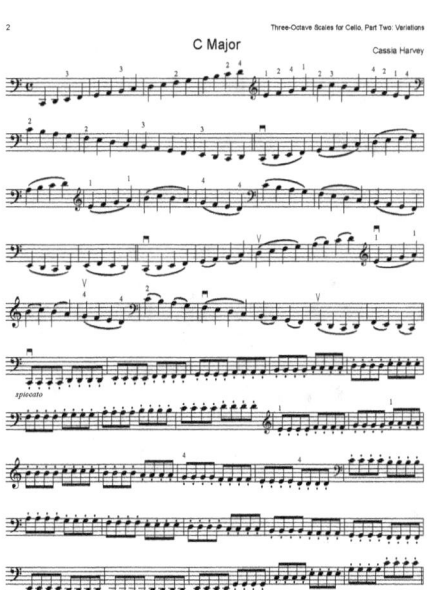

The second book in the *Three-Octave Scales* series gives you numerous left and right-hand variations on the major and minor scales. The variations in this book focus on basic slur patterns, easy spiccato studies, and repetitive rhythm patterns that can help prepare you for encountering scales in repertoire.
CHP271

©2019 C. Harvey Publications All Rights Reserved.

Learning Three-Octave Scales on the Cello

The third book in the *Three-Octave Scales* series gives you more complex variations, including studies in dynamics, multiple spiccato notes in one bow, and exercises to work on left and right-hand agility.
CHP273

This fourth book in the *Three-Octave Scales* series presents complex scale variations for the late-advanced cellist. With extensive work in double stops, sautille, and advanced spiccato, this book gives you daily challenges to help build your technique using the major and minor scales.
CHP316

 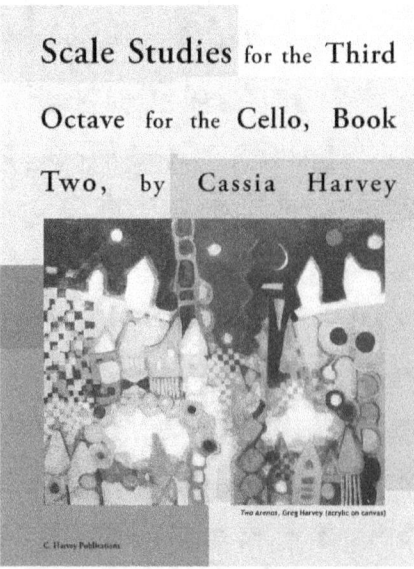

These two books give you exercises that help you shift more precisely in the third (top) octave of major scales. Useful for daily shifting study, these books can help you prepare for playing the scales in auditions.

Mostly in treble clef, these books are most helpful for cellists who already know the notes in the scales.
CHP165, CHP210

©2019 C. Harvey Publications All Rights Reserved.

www.ingramcontent.com/pod-product-compliance
Lightning Source LLC
Chambersburg PA
CBHW051414070526
44584CB00023B/3418